ANIMAL TAG TEAMS

Warthogs and Banded Mongooses

by Kari Schuetz

BLASTOFF!
3
READERS

BELLWETHER MEDIA • MINNEAPOLIS, MN

Note to Librarians, Teachers, and Parents:

Blastoff! Readers are carefully developed by literacy experts and combine standards-based content with developmentally appropriate text.

Level 1 provides the most support through repetition of high-frequency words, light text, predictable sentence patterns, and strong visual support.

Level 2 offers early readers a bit more challenge through varied simple sentences, increased text load, and less repetition of high-frequency words.

Level 3 advances early-fluent readers toward fluency through increased text and concept load, less reliance on visuals, longer sentences, and more literary language.

Level 4 builds reading stamina by providing more text per page, increased use of punctuation, greater variation in sentence patterns, and increasingly challenging vocabulary.

Level 5 encourages children to move from "learning to read" to "reading to learn" by providing even more text, varied writing styles, and less familiar topics.

Whichever book is right for your reader, Blastoff! Readers are the perfect books to build confidence and encourage a love of reading that will last a lifetime!

This edition first published in 2019 by Bellwether Media, Inc.

No part of this publication may be reproduced in whole or in part without written permission of the publisher. For information regarding permission, write to Bellwether Media, Inc., Attention: Permissions Department, 6012 Blue Circle Drive, Minnetonka, MN 55343.

Library of Congress Cataloging-in-Publication Data

Names: Schuetz, Kari, author.
Title: Warthogs and Banded Mongooses / by Kari Schuetz.
Description: Minneapolis, MN : Bellwether Media, Inc., [2019] | Series: Blastoff! Readers. Animal Tag Teams | Audience: Ages 5-8. | Audience: K to grade 3. | Includes bibliographical references and index.
Identifiers: LCCN 2018033935 (print) | LCCN 2018034870 (ebook) | ISBN 9781681036885 (ebook) | ISBN 9781626179585 (hardcover : alk. paper)
Subjects: LCSH: Mutualism (Biology)–Juvenile literature. | Warthog–Behavior–Juvenile literature. | Banded mongoose–Behavior–Juvenile literature.
Classification: LCC QL638.G7 (ebook) | LCC QL638.G7 S388 2019 (print) | DDC 577.8/52–dc23
LC record available at https://lccn.loc.gov/2018033935

Editor: Betsy Rathburn   Designer: Brittany McIntosh

Printed in the United States of America, North Mankato, MN

Table of Contents

A warthog lies down on its side. Soon, a banded mongoose stands on top of the warthog.

It crawls around to pick **ticks** off the warthog's body. The mongoose eats these pests!

5

Warthogs and banded mongooses live in grasslands around Africa.

Tag Team Range

☐ = warthog and banded mongoose range

These animals spend a lot of time in their own **burrows**. But **symbiosis** helps them survive in open spaces.

Wonderful Warthogs

wart

tusk

Warthogs are **mammals** that are related to pigs. They have thick bodies and hairy backs.

Strong **tusks** stick out of their long, flat **snouts**. Large **warts** grow on their faces.

type: mammal
height: 22 to 33 inches (56 to 84 centimeters)
length: 36 to 59 inches (91 to 150 centimeters)
weight: 110 to 330 pounds (50 to 150 kilograms)
life span: up to 15 years

Warthogs are **herbivores**.
They like to **graze** in
grassy areas.

Sometimes, they use their
tusks to dig up roots and other
underground foods.

Banded mongooses are small mammals with long bodies and long tails.

They have light and dark bands across their backs. Sharp, curved claws grow out of their toes.

Banded Mongoose Profile

type: **mammal**
length: **up to 24 inches (61 centimeters)**
weight: **up to 3 pounds (1.4 kilograms)**
life span: **up to 12 years**

The mongooses are not picky eaters. These **carnivores** catch **insects** for most of their meals. But they also hunt larger **prey**.

Sometimes, they even snack on bird eggs!

Helping Each Other

Banded mongooses do not need to hunt when warthogs are near. Warthogs let the mongooses feast on the bugs that cling to their bodies.

The mongooses enjoy
all-you-can-eat dinners!

17

With every mouthful, the mongooses save the warthogs from harmful **parasites**.

These biting bugs cause pain for the warthogs. They can also make the warthogs sick.

Tag Team Trades

warthogs

provide meals

banded mongooses

eat pests

Warthogs and banded mongooses show how friends help one another.

The warthogs provide filling meals. In return, the mongooses get rid of pests!

Glossary

burrows—underground homes where some animals live

carnivores—animals that only eat meat

graze—to feed on grasses

herbivores—animals that only eat plants

insects—small, six-legged animals that have bodies divided into three parts

mammals—warm-blooded animals that have hair and feed their young milk

parasites—living things that use other living things to survive; parasites harm their hosts.

prey—animals that are hunted by other animals for food

snouts—the noses and mouths of some animals

symbiosis—a close relationship between very different living things

ticks—bugs that attach to skin and suck blood; ticks are parasites.

tusks—long, pointed teeth

warts—hard bumps on the skin

To Learn More

AT THE LIBRARY

Carr, Aaron. *I Am A Warthog*. New York, N.Y.: AV2 by Weigl, 2014.

Kipling, Rudyard. *Rikki-Tikki-Tavi*. New York, N.Y.: Morrow Junior Books, 1997.

Zayarny, Jack. *Symbiosis*. New York, N.Y.: Smartbook Media, Inc., 2017.

ON THE WEB

FACTSURFER

Factsurfer.com gives you a safe, fun way to find more information.

1. Go to www.factsurfer.com.

2. Enter "warthogs and banded mongooses" into the search box.

3. Click the "Surf" button and select your book cover to see a list of related web sites.

Index

The images in this book are reproduced through the courtesy of: Travel Stock, front cover (warthog), p. 8; JMx Images, front cover (mongoose top); GUDKOV ANDREY, front cover (mogoose left, middle right, right), pp. 6-7 (mongoose); Utopia_88, front cover (mongoose middle left); SoopySue, pp. 4, 14; Anup Shah/ Nature Picture Library, pp. 5, 20; Patrick Messier, pp. 6-7 (warthog); Aaron Amat, p. 9; David OBrien, p. 10; Panther Media GmbH/ Alamy, p. 11; CarolBeckmann, p. 12; Iakov Filimonov, p. 13; ImageBROKER RM, p. 15; John Waters/ Nature Picture Library, p. 16; Andrew Plumptre/ Getty Images, p. 17; Mark MacEwen/ Nature Picture Library, pp. 18, 21; dawi88888, p. 19 (left); Villiers Steyn, p. 19 (right).